Made in the USA
Monee, IL
13 August 2022

11423536R00070